The One Slap Rule

New Rules for a Happier Society

Daniel W. Orrock

Copyright 2018 by Daniel William Orrock

All rights reserved. No part of this publication may be reproduced, distributed, or transmitted in any form or by any means, including photocopying, recording, or other electronic or mechanical methods without the prior written permission of the publisher, except in the case of brief quotations embodied in the critical reviews and certain other noncommercial uses permitted by copyright law.

Printed in the United States of America

ISBN-13: 978-0-9989496-4-2

10 9 8 7 6 5 4 3 2 1

EMPIRE PUBLISHING

www.empirebookpublishing.com

Illustrations handcrafted by Celestino Galabasa Jr.

Contents

INTRODUCTION 1

CHAPTER ONE
    The Things That Tick Us Off! 5

CHAPTER TWO
    The One Slap Rule! 21

CHAPTER THREE
    Effectiveness of the Slap 28

CHAPTER FOUR
    More Tools of the Trade 34

CHAPTER FIVE
    A Happier Land 47

DISCLAIMER

The One Slap Rule was written purely for entertainment, enjoyment, and laughter. It is primarily based in fantasy, not reality. However, the stories herein are true.

DEDICATION

"This book is dedicated to the three men who taught my large family a very important part of our lives. They taught us how to LAUGH! In loving memory of Ray, Bill, and Jim Orrock, three funny and compassionate men that we will all never forget."

INTRODUCTION

As a young boy growing up Catholic, I learned a great deal from my parents about respect. We called my parent's friends "Mr. Zeller" and "Mrs. Frommelt". We would never dream of calling an adult by their first name. We learned at a very young age to respect our elders.

Do you remember the nuns? I certainly do. The nuns taught us, very quickly, that disrespect would not be tolerated. We lined up. We shut up. We paid attention. Well, we tried to anyway. After all, we were kids, but the bar was set high for us in the respect department.

We have all heard, and maybe experienced the stories about knuckles being cracked with a ruler in school, or ears being pulled toward the bedroom for a time out at home. My least favorite was the hair on the back of my neck being pulled by my saint of a mother. Ouch!

Does this sound harsh? Maybe to some, but I can say that it worked. It got the attention of every young person in the room and the message was clear. Act right, love each other, and be respectful. Our parents, and our nuns, cared about us. They cared about us, and they cared about the future of our society. They taught us respect.

Please consider this excerpt from Forbes.com

"People can be rude, and it appears rude people are on the rise.

After a surge of goodwill among fellow Americans following the Sept. 11, 2001, attacks, manner experts and others have observed a marked drop in courtesy.

One survey commissioned from ORC International by Lenox, a gift company, confirms an increase in such <u>brusque behavior</u>. The survey found more than one-third of 1,000 people polled rate the <u>manners of Americans</u> as poor.

Of course, none of these <u>rude people</u> include ourselves–or so we believe. Most Americans rate their own manners as, well, quite excellent. And therein lies the rub, say etiquette instructors.

"Etiquette is not just about what fork to use," said Sandra Morisset, a professional etiquette trainer in New York City. "It's all about your self-awareness and <u>treating others with respect</u>. If you're not aware of your behavior, that's a problem." Forbes.com 12/4/2003

And this article is years old!

And this excerpt from Time Magazine February 12, 2018

"I'm sorry if this makes me a snowflake, but we find ourselves living at a time of incredible rudeness. Social media has taught the world it needs to have an opinion, on everything, at all times, and that this opinion must be delivered in a forthright way, so we seem assured, confident, smart. Reality television has taught us to celebrate meanness, so long as that meanness is delivered as "honesty" — an awful get-out clause designed by the truly rude so they can say truly rude things and then expect us all to applaud them for it." **By Danny Wallace, Author of "F You Very Much: Understanding the Culture of Rudeness and What We Can Do About It."**

Wow. Isn't that crazy? Human beings are amazing creatures.

I wonder how it would feel to glide through a day never encountering disrespect. How about a lot less of it? How nice would it be to know that the people around you are going to treat you with dignity and actually acknowledge that you matter?

Well, thank God that we have family, friends, and other folks who do just that. But let's face it; there are a bunch of buttheads too. Yes, there is rudeness among us; uncaring, distracted, aloof, and sometimes evil folks who truly get our dander way up.

So, what if rudeness just does happen to show up and say hello? What will we do?

Will we take the high road? Not a bad idea. Will we cave and cry? Sometimes. Will we bite on the insult, lower ourselves, and heave insults? Yes, sometimes.

Or, maybe there is another way. Maybe it's time to FIX that rude individual in a revolutionary way: a way that will lead to a happier, more considerate society.

Think about this. How would it feel to have the answer to rudeness right in your pocket, ready to wield at the next person who really needed fixing?

No, I'm not talking about a knife, or a gun. I'm not talking about a cell phone to take a video or call the police.

I'd like for all of us to consider a fantasyland that might bring our society a ton of peace and laughter; an idea that would require cooperation from everyone. Yes, that's what makes it fantasy. So, let's just roll with it for fun and say that Congress has passed and the President of the United States has signed, legislation that "all will cooperate with this new deal, this new idea, this new law, this new rule for society". Enter the One Slap Rule.

CHAPTER ONE

The Things That Tick Us Off!

We've all seen them, those individuals who don't play nice and couldn't give two rips about the others around them. Sometimes their behavior is simply irritating or a pain in the neck, and other times it is more serious. But let's face it; there are people in this world who, by their rude and thoughtless behavior, tick us off.

There is a multitude of human behaviors that can get under our skin. There is grocery store behavior that is just plain wrong. Sometimes people commit driving infractions that are rude and dangerous. Some people talk loudly on their cell phone in line at the store so that **everyone** can hear their captivating conversation that truly, no one could give two hoots about. Others are simply _mean_. The list goes on and on. Some of these acts are clearly more serious than others but they can all tick us off.

Stop for a minute and think about rudeness in your world.

Who have you encountered, and what have they done that makes you simply shake your head in disbelief or clinch your teeth in anger?

I'm sure that you have a real list of irritants, and I'm confident that we have all encountered the rascal named Rudeness. We would all love to enjoy a society of harmony and respect. Some cultures do it better than others. But let's face it. We have rudeness among us, disrespect among us, angst among us. But we can fix that!

Let's Think About It

I know that when I encounter rudeness or complete selfishness, I am sometimes feeling gracious and I just let things go. And we all know that there are other days (moods) when our tolerance for frustration is waning.

So, before we get into the meat of our glorious One Slap Rule, I want to mention just a few irritants that I have encountered, and that folks I've interviewed have passed along. Can you relate to any of these? How about...

- A fully loaded cart in "10 Items or Less" line. Penalty!
- Unapologetic and hurriedly bumping my shoulder in a crowd.
- Zipping into that parking space **that I am clearly waiting for**. Argh!
- Let that last one sink in.
- Talking **at** me with an Elitist tone. Really? Give me a break!
- Undressing my wife with your eyes **right in front of me!**
- Raising your voice at an employee when the rules don't suit you.
- Being **aloofly unprepared** to order your food when others are waiting. Come on!
- Slow golfers, as if they exist alone on the course.
- Golfers who play music on the golf course. Knock it off!
- Yes, I'm a golfer
- Cell phone conversations on Speaker Phone!
- Meanness toward our elderly, children, or disabled. SLAP!
- Mindless Foul Language in front of kids and others.
- Arrogant SOBs

- People who patronize or belittle others. Ooooo, they're so damn smart.
- "Out of Control" parents at kids sporting events. Grow the hell up.

And of course we have:

- Control Freaks
- Animal Abusers
- Line Cutters
- Loud Talkers
- Slow walkers
- LOUD parenting in public
- Conversation interrupters
- Close talkers
- People who make no eye contact
- LOUD movie goers!
- Blatant liars, Cowards
- Big Phonies, Manipulators
- Disingenuous politicians
- Power abusers
- BULLIES

Yes, yes, yes. And it goes on and on doesn't it? Come on. **Add a few** to the list and shoot me an email at OneSlapRule@gmail.com so I can have a snicker.

And Of Course!

Vehicle Offenses

How many times have you swerved out of the way to avoid an accident? Or how many times have you shaken your head in disbelief as you observe someone's bone headedness in a parking lot or on the road? Let's take a quick look at some road infractions that can tick us off.

- The obvious one of following too closely. Back off, man!
- Going slow in the fast lane.
- Ripping through a parking lot at mach speed.
- Expecting the universe to appease you because you ride a motorcycle. We've seen the looks, the middle fingers, etc. Big baby!
- Cutting people off.
- Merging onto the 65mph freeway going 25mph.
- Driving erratically in and out of traffic or "slingshotting".
- Blinding drivers with the high beams.

- Revving up your damn Harley right next to me at a stop light.
- Aloofly texting while stopped AT A GREEN LIGHT!
- Parking in the Handicapped Parking Area without a permit. Moron!

My good friend Matt had a funny story that he passed along to me the other day. As he pulled into a parking lot to grab a coffee, he noticed his favorite local television personality walking towards the door to Starbucks. Hoping to have a conversation with the television anchor, he parked his car and bee lined to the coffee shop. Boy was he excited.

Well, as he's about to happily enter Starbucks, a woman's voice from behind says, "Sir, can you move your car? I can't open my car door." Matt, bothered because he wants to meet the anchor, obliges the gal and walks back to his car to find it perfectly parked, and the woman's car parked on top of the line, hence her predicament. Well, damn it!

Matt had a number of thoughts going through his head. "You did this to yourself, lady. Why don't you climb through the passenger side? What would Jesus do? I'm gonna miss my opportunity! Damn it, you're ticking me off!"

Well in the end my good friend, being the nice guy that he is, moved his car and ended up having a conversation with his favorite TV anchor. All is well.

But this is yet another example of how people can get our dander up, and fast.

Next up...

Coworker Offenses

Let's not forget these gems of rudeness. Work can be incredibly stressful simply because we are diligent and want to get it right. The natural business obstacles are enough. But now, add a giant ASS to the picture!

Yes, the cocky jerk who loves to gloat, demeans, and blesses you with her passive aggressive statements as she saunters by your desk. What a beauty.

How about:

- The know it all
- The ass kisser
- The "player"
- The drama queen
- Chronic late boy
- The lazy ass
- The office gossip
- The complainer
- The jock that never grew up
- The hovering boss
- The overachiever
- Helpy Helperton
- The ear hustler
- The blame shifter
- The narcissist
- The stress case

Maybe you have a few more to add to the list. Humans are very interesting creatures, aren't they? Now imagine having the solution to your favorite office schmuck right in your pocket, ready to right the wrongs. Hmmm...

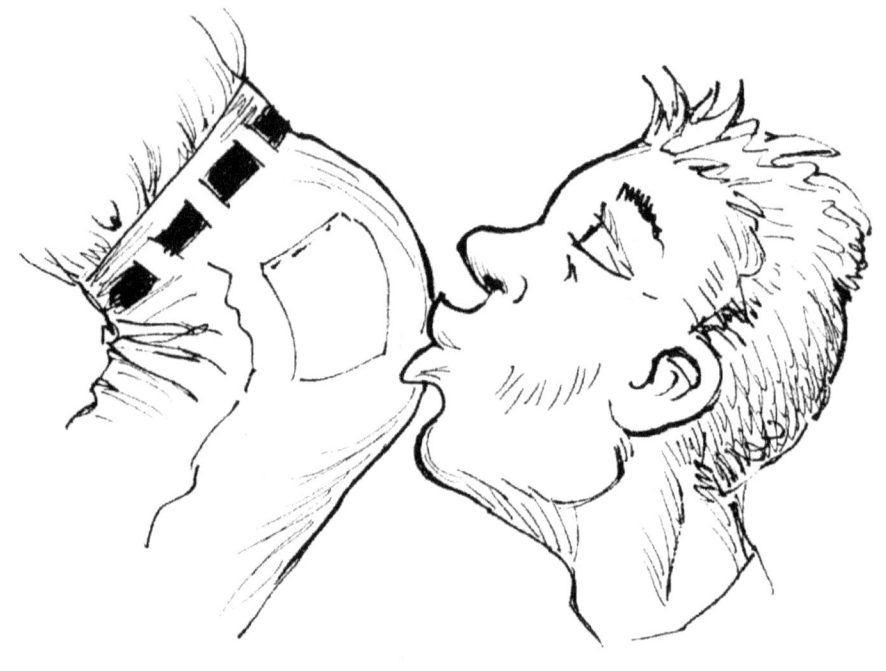

Ok, so let's not forget all of the offenses that occur in our favorite restaurants and hole in the walls across the land.

Restaurant Offenses

It's probably true that wait staff at restaurants have a list of irritants that they encounter as they serve the general public with all of its glorious personalities.

My daughter has been waiting tables for years. She is a good kid and she's a respectful human being. She also has a temper. So, when the drunk, loud- mouthed ass at table two decides to yell at her from across the restaurant to get her attention, boy does he get it!

He also gets her attention when he angrily complains about his meal in front of his guests, God, and the whole restaurant with that A-holish, condescending tone. Good god man is your life that miserable? SLAP!!

Waiters are people; damn hard working people. My daughter and her coworkers would all love to have a thrifty Slap Card ready to dish out to that obnoxious guy or gal who dares to treat them like slaves.

Below are a few restaurant offenses that are very real to the wait staff.

- Cutting off the waiter when he is explaining the specials of the day. Rude.

- Completely ignoring the waiter when greeted, and continuing to converse at the table. Super cool. It's hard to believe that people actually do this. I'm hungry! But straight from a real live waiter, it happens.

- People ordering things that are not on the menu. Read the menu, dude.

- Modifying the hell out of a dish to make it gluten free, and then ordering a beer. Wow! **This is my favorite.**

- Waving the waiter down when he was **just** at your table. By the way, don't wave. Wait, and make eye contact. It's good restaurant etiquette.

- Walking right past the host to seat themselves at a table. Most of the time an uncleared table or a table that has a reserve sign on it.

If you happen to work in a restaurant, you probably have a bunch of irritants that you could add to this list.

Here are a few other restaurant infractions that can affect both staff and patrons.

How about:

- Tipping embarrassingly poorly
- Smacking food
- Loud, loud conversation
- Texting while dining
- Holding a table hostage: good lord, go home!
- Arguing while dining

Yes, they are out there **lurking**, and ready to get our goat. Whether at work, on the road, in the grocery store, the restaurant, or wherever we may be, somebody has the potential to Tick Us Off.

Ok, well I'm pretty sure that you can relate to some of the things that I've mentioned here. It's time to move on to the grand solution for the aloofness, the rudeness, the meanness, and the lack of consideration for others. Now let's have a ball.

CHAPTER TWO

The One Slap Rule!

Let's Be Honest

Here are a couple of statements that you may have made in jest (or not) from time to time. "Man, that guy really needs a slap," or "Dang, I'd love to slap some sense into that rude ass". We don't do it, but we think it, unless of course, you are one of the precious nuns that I mentioned earlier. In that case you'd actually do it. Ha Ha! Just kidding, maybe...

But really, we've all struggled with these thoughts. Wouldn't it be nice to have a structured, agreed upon way to create more peace, rehabilitate the rude, and create a more harmonious land?

Well, here it is my friends. Let's have some fun.

Anatomy of the SLAP!

Are you ready? Here we go. **One time annually** all of us, without penalty, may slap the snot out of somebody who REALLY has it coming.

That's right! We all get a freebie, an ace in the hole, a perfectly orchestrated solution to the rudeness in our society.

Yes, all of us get to open up a sanctioned and perfectly legal "can of whoop-ass" on a jackass who has it coming. Sounds like fun doesn't it?

Imagine for a moment that you are feeling exceptionally *jerky*. You are late for your appointment and you see a parking space that is just perfect for you. Because of course, you're the only person on the planet. But, there's one problem. You're not.

There is actually a sweet, elderly lady stopped with her blinker on, ready to pull into that spot.

You move in for the kill and take that beautiful spot because, after all, you're late for your appointment. (We justify in so many ways).

Now imagine, as you park the car and hurriedly walk past the older lady avoiding eye contact, that a woman approaches you and states,

"Excuse me sir, but you just STOLE that woman's parking space, and it was extremely thoughtless and rude. Please stand still because I'm going to SLAP the snot out of you right here, right now!

Uh oh... This isn't going the way I saw it. I was pretty sure that I could take that spot, avoid eye contact, and weasel my way into my appointment.

Not so fast. You now have a choice to make. You may...

1. **Get the snot slapped out of you** and end up with PRF (puffy red face)

or...

2. **Courteously move your car** for the elderly lady AND apologize.

What Will You Do?

The new rules are at work. You may choose to take the slap and keep it moving as you cooperate with the society's new rules. You're still a jerk, but you just paid for it. Our hope is that after several PRF days you will change your ways.

You may also choose to humbly accept the fact that you acted wrongly. You may move your vehicle, apologize, thank the other woman for pointing it out, make the older woman's day, and feel a hell of a lot better about yourself. PLUS, you'll probably never do it again.

O.S.R.S.

In the One Slap Rule Society (OSRS) there will be no guns, no knives, and no crazy weapons. The people of this new society will live with an expectation that people simply respect others. And if they don't, there will be consequences. Rude people, jerks, giant asses, or any other name you can think of will suffer the consequences of their obtuseness.

In the OSRS the masses are expected to follow the rule of empathy for the good of the entire land. Lack of cooperation with the rule requires that one must suffer the wrath of the polite people. The slap police so to speak. Come on now, don't get too serious. This is gonna be fun!!

The Rules in One Slap Rule Society

1. Everyone in the land will be entitled to one slap per year that will be represented by the "One Slap Card" (OSC) which is unique to every citizen. No buying or trading for more.

2. The slap card has two parts. One part simply states "One Slap", while the bottom part, which is separated by a perforated line, states "Proof of Slap" with the slappee's unique OSR number stamped onto it.

3. Once the Slap Card had been used, the Proof of Slap tab must be sent to the Central Slap Agency (CSA). The CSA will issue a new card in the new calendar year.

4. Slap cards expire upon use, and you may hold onto it for as long as you'd like.

5. Slap cards may only be used for personal offences, and not for fun or retaliation.

6. The Slappee Must Agree To Accept The Slap Without Retaliation.

7. The Slappee is not obligated to listen to a long speech after the slap has been administered. The slap is surely enough. (Snicker...)

8. The Slapper may give two sentences of helpful advice or encouragement after administering the slap.

9. Optional - The **slappee** may choose to display the **slapper's** card, in a place of his or her choosing, as a reminder **to be nice.**

10. Senior citizens, 65 and above, are exempt from the slap.

How to Administer the Slap

After a person has thought through a situation and has decided to make the world a better place, he or she must follow One Slap protocol. The card holder, and future Nobel Peace Prize nominee, must tear off the "Proof of Slap" tab from the card, approach the near future puffy red face slappee, explain why the slap will happen, hand the "slap card" to the slappee, ask that the slappee remain still, and execute slap!

Whack!!!   Yes!

Pretty simple, huh? Public shame, puffy red face, and rehabilitation have begun for the public nuisance. Beautiful.

CHAPTER THREE

Effectiveness of the Slap

Alright, well I hope that you are having some fun and that you have had a few laughs. After all, we've all thought about the Slap from time to time in our hurried, sometimes rude world. So let's talk more about the glorious slap and how it is good for the village.

The Crude 1970s Version

When I was about 13 years old in 1975, I spent a ton of time on my bike riding through town sometimes with my buddies and many times alone. My bike was awesome. It was my transportation and we had a lot fun riding, building high ramps to get as much air as possible, and speeding down open field trails.

On one particular day, I was riding alone, probably on my way to start my paper route at the senior mobile home park. Well, during this period I had learned a new skill. My buddies and I had worked on it. It was called "flipping the bird". It had nothing to do with bikes or ramps or fields. It had everything to do with my middle finger pointing straight up, and in the direction of whomever I chose. It was cool, man.

Well, not on this day! There was a man driving a van down the street and honestly, I can't remember why I chose to use my new skill, but I did. For some reason in my 13 year old brain, it was time for "the bird".

Long story short, I got the snot slapped out of me that day. I remember proudly displaying my finger, and then watching that van come to a screeching halt. I was stunned. Imagine how stunned I was as the man walked over to me and simply slapped me across the head and stated, "Don't ever do that again!" The man got into his van and drove away. WOW! All the fears that go through our minds about this incident and what could have happened. But what DID happen is that I got taught a valuable lesson about disrespect. I still wonder if that man was a nun in disguise.

I'm certainly not making a case for adults randomly slapping teenagers, but the slap worked. It was effective. And, in a controlled, fantasy, One Slap world, it would continue to work. After all you only get One Slap per year. So use it wisely my friends.

There are a couple of reasons why the annual slap can be effective.

Stress Reduction!

Well, I have good news. There is a case to be made here for the One Slap Rule.

Stress reduction is a big one in our fast paced, marketing driven, keep up with the Jones' world that we all attempt to navigate. Raising our kids, building relationships, excelling at work, staying in shape, and many other realities can cause that rascal called STRESS. Now, add to that the expectation from the general public to "always be nice".

According to an article in **Psychology Today**, "what always-nice people tend to do is internalize — hold in negative emotions that naturally rise up in the course of everyday life. The byproducts of these emotional crunches are often depression, anxiety, and addiction". 7/21/2018

Keeping feelings at bay can make a person at risk for acting out in various negative ways including "hurricane-like rages".

Being overly nice can also cause resentment, burnout, and relationship problems simply because a person is not being completely honest about how they feel. They are afraid to "not be NICE".

Harvard Business Review published an article entitled "Beat Generosity Burnout". One of the lines from this article says a lot about being overly nice or generous. It states, "The road to exhaustion is often paved with good intentions". 3/19/2017

Wow! So, there really is evidence that taking off your NICE cap and slapping the snot out of a thoughtless punk, can **really improve your mental health**. Yes! Get excited.

Self Control

The OSR may also produce self control on the part of the slapper. Thought must take place. Think about it. A person offends, maybe even greatly, but will I use my slap card, or will I have mercy, assume the jerk is having a bad day, turn the other cheek (pun intended), or just simply keep moving because I have somewhere to be? Each person controls and guards their slap card carefully. Pick your slap my friends.

Slap Epiphany

It is true that each individual gets only one slap per year, BUT, a jerk may be slapped over and over and over again by multiple slappers as he makes his way through his self absorbed life.

Yes, a person may be slapped, dummy boxed, dummy darted, or slop boxed several times per year. And guess what can happen? Good things can happen.

The proverbial light may just come on, and the numbskull may learn to play nice, have **empathy** for others, and have a hell of lot more peace in his life.

He might want to consider a new way of life; one of respecting other people. Or... he can just continue to be penalized by society and live with puffy red face or huge doses of embarrassment at the grocery store. I tend to think that public shame just might help a person to change his ways for the good of us all.

The Beauty of ONE

I know what you're thinking. We can't go around slapping people for rudeness when we really ought to be able to overlook it or take the high road. Right?

That's why we only get ONE.

The One Slap Rule helps us all to grow up and use our words. But it sure is nice to know that you have that "ace in the hole" in your back pocket just in case you run into "that guy".

Wait a minute! Did you say Dummy Box, Dummy Darts, and a Slop Box?

Well, yes I did, and I'm so happy that you asked. Smirk...

CHAPTER FOUR

More Tools of the Trade

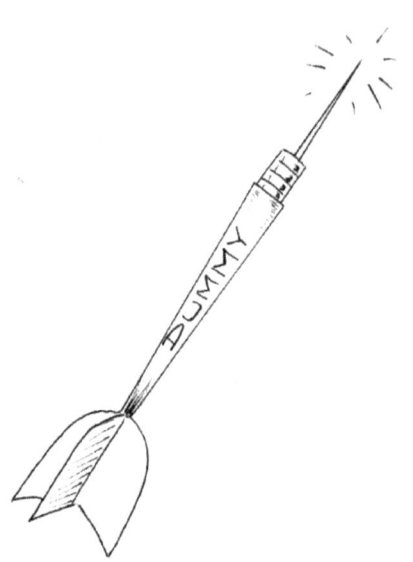 

Introducing...

Dummy Darts

Dummy Darts in a One Slap Society are another annual tool that can be wielded at the completely ignorant and irritating offender.

Imagine that you are driving along at the speed limit with your wife and two grandchildren in the back seat. You are on your way to get lunch and maybe a delicious treat afterward. All is well and it's a beautiful day.

All of the sudden here he comes. Look out, it's a jerk!! The jerk speeds up next to you on the right, looks over at you as if you are a moron, then proceeds to cut you off as he pulls in front of you without using a blinker of course. You have to SLAM on your brakes to avoid a collision. You are startled and your cute little grandkids are now crying in the back seat.

The fears of what "could" have happened go through your head. Your wife puts on her protection hat, and she is now in **full on** grizzly bear momma mode. Momma's ready to kick some butt!

The jerk sneers at you in his rear view mirror, and then proceeds to roll down his window and do my favorite 13 year old thing. He flips you "The Bird".

We've all seen them; the angry, dangerous, bird-flipping, bad drivers.

What will you do?

Here's what you can do. DUMMY DART the SOB!!!

That's right. A **dummy dart** is for dummies who put other people's lives in danger with their ignorant self-absorption and their giant piece of metal, glass, plastic, and rubber; sometimes known as a car or a truck.

How Dummy Darts Work

A dummy dart is an annual one-use projectile that you may shoot at a vehicle when the driver of that vehicle is being a giant ass. The dummy dart is simply a loaded magnet that, when attached to the car, immediately shuts down that car, disabling it where it sits for a period of 30 minutes, just enough time for the offender to ponder the situation and grow the hell up.

The car manufacturers in this One Slap World have agreed to place the technology in every vehicle in order to make this work. And believe me. It Works!

Imagine the joy of Dummy Darting the person that has your wife so upset and your sweet grandchildren crying in the back seat.

You administer the dart and the vehicle comes to a stop. You drive by and wave with a smile. Your grandchildren even wave. Your wife is satisfied.

Now here comes the real fun. Public Shame!

Yes, public shame. All of the cars behind you must now go around you and your dummy-darted car. They shout shaming words at you like, "dummy!!" as they drive by. Multiple people are now inconvenienced by your rude dumbness. Sound too harsh? Not as harsh as a destroyed car with a man, his wife, and their two grandchildren inside.

The Dummy Dart has done its work. It has caused a 30 minute delay in this man's life. He has been publicly shamed by the "Village". And he now has a trophy that he may choose to display in a place of his liking to remind him of the thoughtlessness that greatly offended and could have hurt somebody.

After a few of these, I do believe that the proverbial light will appear, a little angel on his shoulder, and this man will become a more thoughtful and safe driver. He will also feel better about himself and his positive contribution to society.

And now we move on to another fantastic tool in the OSRS.

The Dummy Box

Imagine that you are grocery shopping and you notice that a person has put a head of lettuce where the corn is. They have already touched it with potentially dirty hands, and they are simply too lazy to walk it back 30 feet to the lettuce section. Grocery store infraction!

What if you had 10 items in your basket and have decided to check out. You walk happily up to the "10 Items or Less" line and see a man unloading his FULL basket onto the food escalator. Yes, the other lines are packed, and he should be standing in one of them. But, he ain't! This is a big time grocery store infraction. The grocery checkout clerk has a part in this one too.

Wait! Did you see that woman pick her nose (or something '; [else, yikes) and proceed to put her bare hand into the mixed nut bin? In the words of Jimmy Fallon, EW! I mean **EW**!!!

I actually witnessed this one; an aloof man, proudly walking his nasty, wing-flapping, giant **parrot** down the produce isle as if to proudly contaminate all of our produce. Wow. Just wow.

And let's not forget the gal who lets her four children act like wild savages as they race loudly through the store running into carts, people, everything.

What about that jerk running at 50 mph to cut in front you in line? Or the line that a sweet elderly lady is about to get into? Infraction!

I'm sure you have your Grocery Store Infraction pet peeves.

Well, the Dummy Box is the answer. The dummy box is another form of public humiliation with the aim to correct self-centered behavior and make our world a much happier place.

The Setup

Well, each grocery store will have an elevated dummy box in the center of the store which can be **seen by all** when a dummy is on display.

The store will also have Grocery Infraction Police (GIP) who will be available to receive complaints from customers who have observed an infraction. The store surveillance video or other witnesses will suffice as proof of the dummy's behavior.

The offender will be escorted to the dummy box by the GIP. He then must walk up the staircase as special **"dummy infraction music"** plays for all to hear and see. Yes, the shaming has begun.

Wait, we can't have that happen without the proper head attire. I almost forgot about the dunce cap. Yes! We've all heard of it. Now we can see it on full display as the offender stands on the platform wearing the dunce cap with the music playing as people walk by and little children point and laugh.

I'm pretty sure the proverbial light will come on after that embarrassing moment. Dang, I'll never do **THAT** again in a grocery store.

Restaurant Slop Box

The One Slap society has a special penalty for bad restaurant behavior too. If a jerk, or his battle axe wife, decides to treat one of our awesome wait staff like a slave, or commits other restaurant infractions, the Restaurant Infraction Police (RIP) will escort the offender promptly to the slop box. The Slop Box is a wonderfully sloppy place specially designed for folks who behave poorly in our dining establishments.

The Slop Box is a loud and lively spot where restaurant patrons, the polite ones, gather together to throw large amounts of food at the ass in the story, as he stands with his hands resting courteously at his sides, soaking up the slop. Imagine this. Lettuce, steak scraps, half-eaten bread, pasta, and blops of butter will be the dummy's new wardrobe. How about a little alfredo sauce with that? Ha! What an awesome picture!

It's called the Slop Box because when the polite diners are done with rude boy, he's going to be a sloppy mess. And after all of the fun, as he takes the walk of shame through the restaurant and into the Slop Shower in the back of the restaurant, the restaurant patrons will all laugh in unison. Yes, he will be reminded of his rudeness and his need to be a nicer person. I don't ever want to be "slopped"!

The Dummy at the Doctor's Office

Before we move on to the Double or Triple Dose, I'd like to share with you an event that I encountered personally; something that I will never, ever forget for reasons that will soon become very clear. Once upon a time there was a man who was in the X-ray department at the hospital. This man clearly had a problem with patience.

The sweet receptionist checked him in and got him straight back to the MRI area of the clinic. The man had taken some prescription drugs to ease the claustrophobia of the MRI procedure.

Well, there happened to be a couple of **emergencies** that trumped this man's appointment and caused him to have to wait. Wow. What a concept. Wait.

The man was not happy and began to complain to every staff member within ear shout. Finally, donning his handsome patient gown and underwear, and drugged from the medication, he decided to go out to the reception area, shuffle through all of the other patients in the waiting room with his **butt crack showing**, and rant to the polite receptionist about his frustrations, something that was totally out of her control.

Then this man, because of his inability to wait, simply left the clinic without getting his procedure. He offended some hard working folks, didn't get the treatment that he needed, and threw a wrench into the clinic's schedule.

Well, that man was me! Yes, I was the moron that day and I'm not proud of it. Can you believe it? I was that guy, dang it.

My wife witnessed the whole thing. But I escaped without having the **snot slapped out of me**, which I am very thankful for. I did reflect on my actions and have realized the error of my ways thanks to my wonderful wife.

But, in a One Slap society, things could have gone very differently for me and I may have had to learn my lesson in a One Slap way. I am confident that a good dose of One Slap reality would have gotten me on the right track. Yes, it would have been extremely **effective**.

The Double or Triple Dose!

This is really exciting to think about. Yes, get excited. You may be able to seriously teach the biggest ASS you've ever encountered with the Double or Triple Dose.

This next story actually happened to a friend of mine, Darian.

Imagine pulling into the grocery store parking lot. You see a car pull into a handicapped parking spot and then watch as a young man and woman race to the store entrance. There is no handicapped sticker on the license plate and no placard hanging in the window. And, since your dear uncle, who you care for daily, is disabled, you are especially bothered by this.

Well, the rest of the story goes like this.

Darian, my friend, approached the two young adults in the store and inquired about the parking spot. He asked if they had a placard that they could place in the window, and explained that these spots are very important to folks who suffer from a disability.

The woman proceeded to tell Darian to mind his own business and "f*** off". Darian, who was shocked, stated "what"? The woman made some more profane comments and proceeded to tell my African American friend that she didn't talk to nig***s. Can you believe it?

The woman was loud, obnoxious, racist, and witnessed by a group of other shoppers. What a piece of work.

Long story short, she and her wimpy companion were removed from the store by the Grocery Infraction Police and told to never come back.

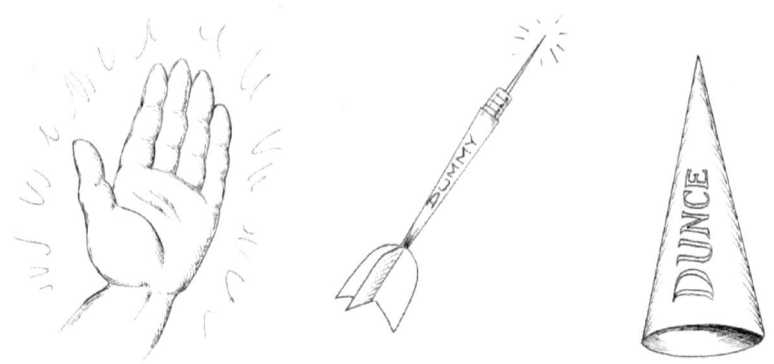

So, what we have here is a barrage of offenses. We have a vehicle violation. Dummy Dart! We have a racist grocery store violation. Dummy Box!! Then, just because of this woman's rudeness, you may top it all off with a righteous SLAP. Ha!

Yes, it is at this point that you may employ the **Triple Dose**. This may just turn a Giant Bonehead into a saint. What a concept! You may dummy dart, dummy box, and slap the snot out of a jerk and then send them on their merry way.

The village has spoken. Hopefully this gal, after being publicly humiliated in the Dummy box, suffering from Puffy Red Face, and sitting in a towed car that won't move, will reflect on her actions and decide to be a nicer human being.

Or, she can just live a life of PRF. It's up to her.

CHAPTER FIVE

A Happier Land

Yes, a happier land. I think all of us would love a happier land.

Many world religions and philosophies agree on certain points that are worth noting, and that throughout history have made people happier and more content. And let's face it; there is a lack of contentment in our world. We all strive to find contentment in SO many ways.

People may disagree on many things, and on ways to find contentment. But on these few gems, I think that most humans can agree with, and benefit from.

1. Follow the Golden Rule of treating people like we'd like to be treated.

2. Genuinely care about and help the downtrodden in our world.

3. Be mindful of our actions and "think it through".

4. Positively contribute and interact with our communities.

5. Take responsibility for our actions.

Angry Jesus

Let's take a quick detour from the gems mentioned above, and think about a bit of history that isn't talked about much.

Even Jesus got ticked!!

Recorded in the Christian book, the Bible, is this passage:

*"And **Jesus** went into the **temple** of God, and cast **out** all them that sold and bought in the **temple**, and <u>overthrew the tables</u> of the money changers, <u>and the seats</u> of them that sold doves."*

Yes, the Man who history records as a teacher and model of kindness and acceptance **totally went off** on a group of people that he perceived as disrespectful. He was tossing tables and chairs!

I can hear someone saying in a whiny voice "Well, damn, that doesn't sound very nice".

Exactly! But it was effective, and he didn't have to bury his frustrations deep down. He handled it. He got it out. Even Jesus wasn't *always nice*. And I'll bet that he felt better after taking care of business. He confronted the bad behavior. Confrontation might not feel wonderful at the time, but in the end we feel better for doing the right thing and hashing it out. We are happier.

My dear mother-in-law Rita, bless her heart, had a sign in her home that read, "I Yell Because I Care!" Classic.

Well, I second that motion. "I Slap Because I Care!"

In our new One Slap Society, as the years roll on, puffy red face, dummy darts, the dummy box, and the slop box will be the norm for certain folks who just can't seem to get it right. However, over time, the new rules will have their desired effect and people will continue learning and growing. They will be happier.

A lot of folks will be **happier**, simply because they have expressed themselves and have righted some wrongs. Some folks will be **happier** because they have had the slap epiphany and have decided to live a better life. And some folks will be **happier** because some giant ass didn't steal their parking space. Yes!

And, as the years go by, the **hope** is that the Slap, the Dart, and the Box will bring the plan to fruition and that there will be a hell of a lot more smiles, hugs, and handshakes. Wouldn't that be awesome? It certainly is fun to imagine.

Yes, our imaginations can take us in a gazillion different directions. It's amazing what our minds can dream up and it's a real blessing to have it.

The idea for the One Slap Rule has developed over time as my brother, my sisters, and I have talked it over and laughed loudly as we let our imaginations run wild. Our family is fortunate to have had a father and a mother who raised us with a large sense of humor. It's the good stuff. And it sure has been a blast thinking through the One Slap Rule.

But in the end, I believe that we all just want to move about in society with genuine care and empathy as the ruling lights. And, when we see the **opposite** of that, we wish it wasn't there. But hey, we live in a real world that just ain't perfect.

Hopefully, as we think about the idea of the One Slap Rule, we will grow to do some things better and to do our part in creating this happier land.

1. Maybe we can all get better at using our words to explain to others *exactly how* they were ridiculously rude, <u>without</u> resorting to our annual slap.

2. Maybe we can learn to be empathetic towards others who may just be having a rough time of it. In fact, confronting bad behavior in a polite way may open the door for humanity to take place. We never know what somebody is going through.

3. And maybe, being a **slap recipient** will encourage us to start thinking more about others as we consider them and not ourselves so much.

HOWEVER in the end, if it happens to be that day when the inconsiderate jerk is unwilling to see the error of his ways, **well...**

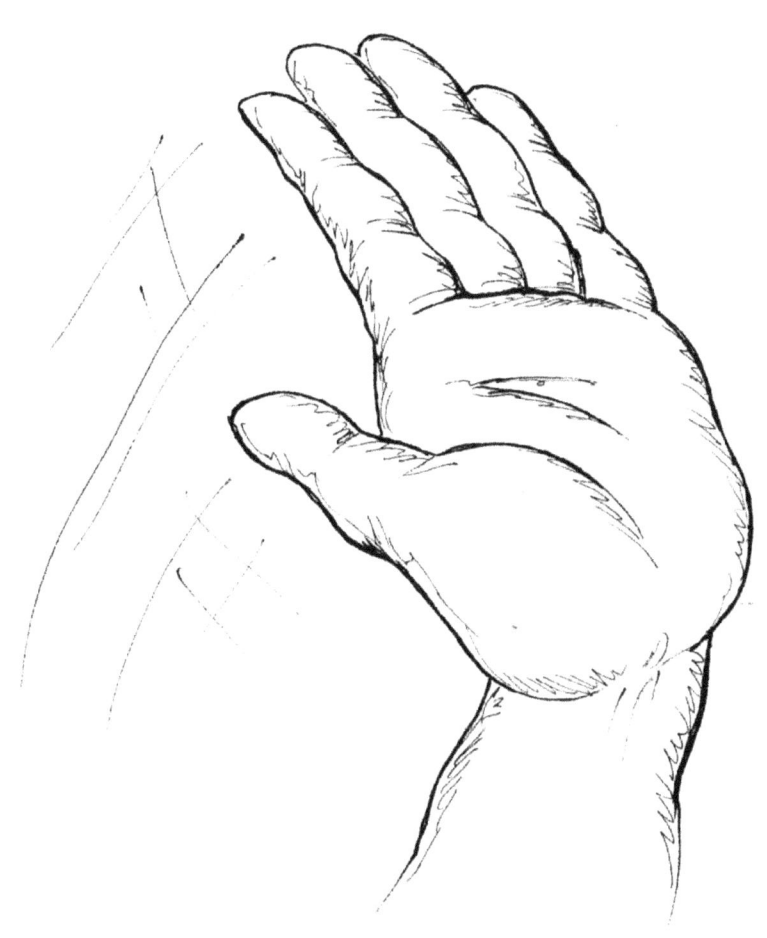

About the Author

Daniel W. Orrock resides in Northern California with his beautiful wife, Jeanie. In his career working for the State of California Dan, as often as possible, used humor to interact with others and to create a less toxic environment.

Dan co-managed a youth diversion program that assisted misguided young men and women in finding the right path through better decision making. He learned a lot by simply listening to the stories of those young people.

He is also an aspiring musician who plays guitar, attempts to sing, writes songs, and enjoys many different music genres.

Dan and Jeanie have four hardworking children and are the proud "Papa" and "Gramma" of four wonderful grandchildren, with one on the way.

www.ingramcontent.com/pod-product-compliance
Lightning Source LLC
Chambersburg PA
CBHW050448010526
44118CB00013B/1729